THE THIRD KISS
A COMEDY IN ONE ACT BY AUSTIN CLARKE
DOLMEN EDITIONS XXIV

ISBN 0 85105 292 4

Printed in Ireland

Characters

PIERROT *as* PETER BLAKE

PIERRETTE *as* PAULINE QUINN

HARLEQUIN

FATHER DOYLE

GENTLEMAN IN AN OPERA CLOAK

All enquiries regarding performing and other rights should be made to the Permissions Department, The Dolmen Press Limited, North Richmond Industrial Estate, North Richmond Street, Dublin 1.

PROLOGUE

(Dressing-room at the Abbey Theatre in 1913. Screen upstage, left, behind which Pierrette is changing costume. Another screen, opposite, right, on which Pierrot's jacket is hanging. Two chairs, on one of which Pierrot is sitting in his shirt sleeves. He wears ordinary trousers and is pulling up his socks.)

PIERRETTE *(calling)*
    Pierrot.

PIERROT   What is it, dear?

PIERRETTE *(backing out)*   The back of my bodice,
    Unhook it, please.

PIERROT *(He stretches to do so, admiring.)*
                You have a real body!

PIERRETTE
    I am a human being now: no longer
    A type.

    (She turns round.)

PIERROT   Somehow, your arms and legs are longer.

PIERRETTE   And yours.
                What can it mean?

PIERROT *(coming closer)*   The better to hold
    Each other, when there is nothing to withhold.

    (She smiles, turns quickly. He unhooks all bodice.)

    Your new back is so beautiful!

PIERRETTE *(turning)*   I'm scared,
    Pierrot, to go upon the stage, can scarcely
    Breathe.

PIERROT   Draw deeper. We are real at last.

(bows, miming)

A birthday present.

PIERRETTE   What is it?
PIERROT   A pair of elastic —
Pink — garters.

(She pretends to accept.)

                    Let me come and put them on
For you, Miss Quinn.

PIERRETTE   Sir, not upon my honour!

(She retires behind screen. Pierrot puts on collar, knots
tie several times, looking in mirror off stage. Goes
behind screen for tie pin. Puts it in, then runs over
some of his lines.)

PIERROT (acting)
'Her name and address are printed in The Evening
Mail'
          da-da
                    'Number eleven Dominick
Street'
          da-da-da-
                    'At the tram-stop?'
                              da-da-da
Cue
          'Into a convent?
                    'But you're safe now'

(Repeats run through)

PIERRETTE (calling)
I cannot hear a word. What are you saying?

8

It sounds to me like da-da, da-da, da.
Sense ripped from canvas: they'll call it Dadaism.

PIERROT   You're wrong, Pierrette. I'm only studying
My lines.

(*aside, feeling neck*)

O damn. I hate this collar and stud.

(*He puts on coat and cap.*)

PIERRETTE (*coming out*)
I'm ready. How do you like my hat and blouse,
Tailor-made skirt?

PIERROT   They match cap, coat and trousers.

PIERRETTE   What's wrong, dear?

PIERROT   Too many underclothes for petting.
Corset

— or stays —

camisole,

petticoat

(*pulling up her skirt*)

Big drawers.

PIERRETTE   Pierrot, you should not misbehave.
Have you forgotten we are human beings
To-night?

PIERROT   New, pretty ancle . . .

another peep,

Pierrette,

PIERRETTE   Not now. We are respectable people
According to the play —

PIERROT   Unhappy,

PIERRETTE (*sadly*)   Tormented
   By conscience,

PIERROT   Fear of sin.

PIERRETTE   The author meant
   The play, perhaps, to be satiric

PIERROT   They call
   It — 'Realism',

   (*Pierrette starts to complete her make-up at mirror.
   Voice off*)

PIERRETTE   Hurry, there's the first call.

PIERROT   I know my lines.

PIERRETTE   I hope the lighting cues
   Will be on time.
               (*turning*)
                     Pierrot, I am so curious
   About that scene, off stage. What happens at the verge
   Of the dark wood?

PIERROT   I dare not tell a virgin!

   (*stage darkens*)

PIERRETTE (*alarmed*)
   What is it?

PIERROT   Lower your voice, dear.
                                 Harlequin's
   Outside.

PIERRETTE (*indignantly*)
         Last night he said I would have quins.

PIERROT
    Last week he boasted to me :
                        'I am an air-
    Demon' and swore his baton was an heirloom
    From Hell. They say he was a mediaeval
    Vice in Cathedral plays —

PIERRETTE   Acrobat, meddler —

PIERROT
    And ran with fire on St. Bartholomew's Eve
    By Paris courtyard, terror — smoking mews,
    The ball-and-powder men, the pike-men, massacred
    Thousands of people who never went to Mass,
    Huguenots with their wives and children, hacked
    To bits or trampled on by frightened hackneys,
    That steel-lit night Coligny was condemned
    For treason and with him the young Prince of Condé,
    No bolt or bar, portcullis clang, could keep that
    Air-demon out of palace or down in keep.

    (*warning*)

    He's spangling in the shadows.

    (*Lights up. Harlequin, masked, stands between the
    screens.*)

PIERRETTE   Harlequin !

HARLEQUIN
    Good evening, Blake.
                    How do you do, Miss Quinn ?
    You look so innocent on your arrival
    In Dublin's fair city.
                    Have I still a rival
    For that last favour ?

PIERROT   The self-same harlequinade,
    Back to the bugled camp, the cannonade, the . . .

HARLEQUIN   One moment, please.
                    (*To Pierrette*)
                    We'll meet in the second scene.
    Off stage, the human mind is quite obscene.

    (*He leaves*)

PIERROT
    Don't cry, Pierrette. I'll tumble down the props,
    Prevent him from doing anything improper,
    Thwack him with his own baton.

PIERRETTE (*musing*)   I wonder what
    It's like?

PIERROT (*puzzled*)   What, dear?

PIERRETTE   A mortal kiss.

PIERROT   We'll try one.

PIERRETTE   Not yet. I'm nervous.
                        After the curtain rises,
    We'll steal one.

PIERROT   But the author —

PIERRETTE   We'll take a rise
    Out of him.

PIERROT   Suppose that something happens.

PIERRETTE (*laughing*)
    We'll risk all, give his play a happy ending.

    (*Second call. They hurry off.*)

CURTAIN

SCENE ONE

(Night. St. Mary's Place, Dublin. Gas-lamp, right; Apse of the 'Black Church'; back stage, Peter Blake and Pauline Quinn are standing near the lamp-post. He opens a newspaper.)

PETER
    Her name and address are printed in *The Evening Mail*.

PAULINE   Do let me see them, Peter.
    (reading)   'Miss Eve
    O'Leary.'

PETER   'Number Eleven Dominick Street.'

PAULINE
    Our Lady of Good Counsel saved her in the nick
    Of time, when she was going home from the Tech
    The other night. She told me she saw a detective
    Half hidden in the shadows at Fenelley's Hardware
    Store. As she passed, he said 'I beg your pardon,
    Miss.' To her horror it was a fellow wearing
    A raincoat. Before her Angel could whisper 'Beware!,
    Don't look!', she turned, caught her miraculous medal,
    Her mother o' pearl beads blessed by the Pope — and
            fled
    Back from the corner to the little sweet-shop
    Near Downes' Bakery.

PETER   At the tram-stop?

PAULINE   Yes —
    It's open till half-past ten. She almost fainted,
    Forgot the name of Imelda, her patron saint. Then
    Somebody brought a kitchen chair to the counter

Where she could hear a big clock slowly counting
Each heart-beat. When she recovered, Mrs. Holme-
     patrick
Got one of the bigger lads to bring her home.
Four other girls and a married woman had seen
That man. The married woman made such a scene,
He showed his heels.
(*shivering*)   Peter, I am afraid.
They noticed that the cuffs of the raincoat were
     frayed.

(*turning to him*)

Why is the world mysterious with evil?

PETER   No need to be upset.

PAULINE   I want to leave it,
   Go into a Mercy Convent.

PETER (*playfully*)   But you're safe now,
   I'll be your banker, hide you in my safe. A
   Kiss will unclick the combination lock,
   But you must keep my snapshot in your locket.
   (*coaxing*)
   We'll try that key.

PAULINE   Peter, it wouldn't be right.
   Remember what I told you last Thursday. I'll write
   To you. Before our tea, I was stitching a doyley
   For Mother — and thought of the words that Father
         Doyle said
   To me. I may be chosen for a religious
   Vocation. I must be patient, pray, rely
   On Heaven.

PETER   Why did you go to that Jesuit Chapel
    In Gardiner St.? I know a quiet chap
    Who went there. Now, he fancies he has a light
    Around his head.
    (*humming*)   'All passengers alight,'
    The tram-conductor sang, 'Trolley's alight!'

PAULINE   O do be serious. The people say
    That Father Doyle must surely be a saint.

    (*relenting*)

    I'm very sorry, dear. I do not mean
    To be unkind — and yet I feel so mean.
    Please, take me home.

PETER (*miming, aside*)   Not yet. I have a note
    From the dressing-room.

    (*he winks*)

PAULINE (*pretending to read it*)
    But somebody might notice.

PETER   We'll hide.

    (*Back stage dims as they come forward to extreme
    left. Moonlight, front stage. They kiss.*)

PIERRETTE (*withdrawing off stage*)
    What have you done to me, my Pierrot?

PIERROT (*following her*)
    Just improvised a scene!

    (*They come back. He is wearing a 'boater', she has a
    large straw hat.*)

PIERRETTE   We're on a pier. O
    Look at the wavelets!

PIERROT   And the gigantic wheel,

PIERRETTE   The switch-back,

PIERROT   Swingboats

PIERRETTE   Up.

PIERROT   Down

PIERRETTE   — like your tickles.
   I think it must be Blackpool

PIERROT   Or New Brighton.

PIERRETTE   It could be Coney Island.

PIERROT   The moon is bright on
   Your hair.
   (*miming*) Come for a stroll along the Prom, Miss,
   The last time we held hands you made a promise
   To meet me in Southend.

PIERRETTE   That telegram
   You sent! A double-room in the big Hotel
   On the Front. They called it *The Majestic*.

PIERROT   First, you said 'no'.

PIERRETTE   I thought it only a jest.
   (*dreamily*)
   And then.

PIERROT   Remember the next morning. Mud
   For miles. The tide was out.

PIERRETTE   I was so muddled
   By want of sleep.
                         I brought a bathing costume.

PIERROT   We couldn't dip.

16

PIERRETTE   Red and blue stripes. It cost
     A lot.

PIERROT   We looked in shops,

PIERRETTE   Penny bazaars —
     With slot machines.

PIERROT (*miming*)   *Parade of the Hussars* —

PIERRETTE   Played on a phonograph.

PIERROT   And then the Palm-Grove.
     A fortune-teller read your small white palm.

PIERRETTE   And you were jealous.

PIERROT   She knew the hidden lines
     Of destiny.
                      'Where are my marriage lines?'
     You asked.

     (*they laugh*)

PIERRETTE   We saw the Strong Man show his muscles

PIERROT   Fat Lady

PIERRETTE   Ate whelks and shrimps.

PIERROT   Collops

PIERRETTE   — and mussels

PIERROT   We met again in Wapping
                              Or was it Stepney?

PIERRETTE   Two 'one-and-one's' —

PIERROT   Ray.

PIERRETTE   Whiting.
  (*alarmed*)   I hear a step.

  (*they listen*)

PIERROT   You're right. Someone is coming from Dorset
         Street.

  (*The back of the stage lights up.*)

  (*aside*)
  We're in the play. I recognise the setting.

  (*They retire, come back, with cap and hat, stand by
  lamp-post.*)

PAULINE (*aside*)
  You say that little rhyme. I answer promptly.

PETER   I can't remember it

PAULINE (*whisper*)   I'll try to prompt

PETER (*coming forward*)
  Run, run around the Black Church in St. Mary's Place.

PAULINE   *Three times at night.*

PETER   *— and see the Devil,*

PAULINE   *Face —*

PETER   *to face.*

PAULINE   We played that local game when we were
         children
  One wintry night.

PETER   Our legs and arms were chilled.

PAULINE   We challenged Tom Delaney, Lily Gaynor.

18

PETER   The first time round, the pair of us were gaining.

PAULINE   I tripped. You picked me up.
    (*pointing*)   Terrible echoes
Were stirring in that Protestant Church.

PETER   A second
   Time round.

PAULINE   A third —

PETER   Without a handicap
   And we were leading

PAULINE   Then you lost your cap,
   The others passed us by.

PETER   A double scream.

PAULINE   We found poor Lily sobbing.
    (*laughing*)   They had seen
   A small black cat.

PETER   We heard that young Delaney
   Outbawled

PAULINE   — by echoes —

PETER   down the nearest lane.

PAULINE   I think it really was the Devil.

PETER   We'll play
   That game again.

PAULINE   I daren't

PETER (*aside*)   It's in the play.
   Give me your hand. You did it once before.
   When you had two long plaits, white pinafore.

(*thoughtfully*)
They fit the conscience on when boot and shoe
Are smaller. In vain our commonsense cries 'shoo'!

PAULINE (*yielding reluctantly*)
O what will Father Doyle say?

(*They run off left, down stage. Footsteps fade. Pause.
A distant church clock strikes. They enter up stage,
right.*)

PETER   Second lap!

(*Steps fade. Sound of horse-and-cab comes near, fades.
Steps again. The pair run in. She stops.*)

PETER   Come on.

PAULINE   I thought I heard a cat.

PETER (*pointing right*)
                                        He's lapping
A hellish saucer over there; sulphuric
Acid: His whiskers smoking, eyes — furious.
(*smiling as she retreats*)
I'm only joking.
                    Come, a last endeavour.

(*They run off. A gentleman in opera cloak steps from
the shadows and stands, smoking a cigarette, beside
the lamp-post.*)

PAULINE (*off*)
I'm winning.
(*She runs in.*)

GENTLEMAN (*saluting*)
Good evening, Miss.

(*He turns, showing devil-mask*)

20

PAULINE   The Devil!

(*Screams, runs off, left. The stranger signs to the lamp.
The flame goes out. He vanishes. Peter runs in.*)

PETER (*frightened*)
    She screamed.
                        I cannot find her in the dark.
    The street-lamp is out.
                        Pauline, where are you? —

VOICE OF PAULINE (*echoing far off*)   Are you?

(*Low drumming. Black out.*)

CURTAIN

SCENE TWO

(*Edge of a wood. Evening time. Fr. Doyle enters, left. Stage gradually dims.*)

FR. DOYLE

Why do you follow me with torment, hide
Beneath a blessed robe that scalding hide,
Murmur impurities — confession door
Cannot hold back? I hear angels adore
At midnight, then feel under my stomach-pit
Temptation stir, rising again.

                                   God pity
Me, now and forever, aid me to win back
My self. Have I not waited all the winter
To crush a cure out of the nettle-seed,
Called on a heaven of saints to intercede
For me and gained so many indulgences
I cannot count them — mind has got so dull?
All dusty green and grey; the stings have grown.
I'll roll my pain in them without a groan.
Can penitential suffering be rash?
Burn in me, nettles, nettles. Every rash
That spreads along my skin will multitude
The purgatory.
(*looking round*)   Horribly thewed
And loined, you still confront me bodily, stare
To stare, ambush, salute me, on a stair
Or landing.

                I'll imitate the holy follies,
Be wise, burn, itch in pore, in follicle:

(*murmuring, off*)

Escape the daily conversation, tight-lipped.

(*Stage in darkness. Voices press around him.*)

22

VOICES

    'Come, Father Doyle, you've lost your

                                    appetite'

'No soup, to-day?'

                  'A scrap of beef?'

                                'You trifle

With knife, fork?'

                 'Let me help you to some trifle.'

'Rice pudding?'

          'Tapioca?'

                 'Have you read

The latest speech in the Commons by Mr. Redmond?
The Freeman's Journal has a stirring leader
On it to-day denouncing the British leader.'
'Tell us your dream, now, Father Tompkins?'

                           'Three boys were

Sent up for punishment. They had been boisterous
In Latin class. The third was found cogging.
A water-pistol, apples, pennies, snot-rags,
Toffee, wire-springs, came tumbling out of their
            trouser
Pockets, three sticks of chalk, handballs. I trounced
            them
So hard, I wakened up. Though all was still,
I could have sworn I heard the bare strapping still,
Then glanced at the luminous dial of my watch,
The time — a quarter to four!

FR. DOYLE   Why does he watch me
Like that across the refectory table?

(*Light comes up*)

(*repenting*)
God help me, my thoughts have been uncharitable.

                                            23

(turning)
I see it all. Another trick. You tempt,
Try to delay me, from my first attempt to
Use an old discipline : The nettle-bed
Our ancient hermits lay in.
                                    That nettles you!

(Light has been increasing)

(bewildered, searching)
Dear me! Where did I put my gloves, my scarf?
I must protect face, hands, from blister, scar.

(He draws them from his pockets, hurries off, right, up stage.)

(A long pause. Laughter off. Peter enters.)

PETER *(calling back)*
Quick, mind the cowpats there.

PAULINE *(entering, beating back swarm)*
                                    Those dreadful flies
Buzzing, darting around us. Hundreds of
Them.

PETER *(pointing)*
                    Cows grazing.

PAULINE   That's it. I had a feeling
That I was here before. Yes, this is the field
And there's the wood. It seems so long ago.
Molly O'Brien, Teresa and I were going
For a walk in the high grass beneath the hedgerows.
Teresa ran on to pluck a bramble rose.
While we were searching for honeysuckle, we heard
Her give a cry of terror, saw a herd
Of cattle lying down. A red cow had

Got up. We laughed, called her a great big coward,
But when she dared us to go into the wood :
Afraid of being afraid, we said we would.
The darkness fluttered. We rushed out, past an old
shed,
The nettles stinging our legs.
                              The tears we shed !

(*suddenly, puzzled*)

I'm tired — as if I had been running.

PETER   Sit down
And rest —
(*smiling*)
            before this field becomes a city
Street.

(*They sit on a grassy bank.*)

PAULINE (*puzzled*)
      Why are we here, Peter ? There must be a reason.

PETER   You came here once with Molly O'Brien, Teresa.

PAULINE (*softly*)
The honeysuckle, wild roses, we never picked.
(*searching her handbag*)
It's like a dream that I had a holy picture
For you.
            It's gone !

PETER (*jumping up, searching his pockets*)
                  I had our tram-fare back.
Gone, too !

(*sits down, depressed*)
            I think we came . . . to say farewell.

PAULINE   Yes. . . .
   But we love each other. Why should we part?

PETER   Some power beyond us plays another part.

PAULINE   This human life is such a mystery.

PETER   I'll borrow more books on science, find the missing
   Link, search the large *Encyclopedia
   Britannica.*
                    Dread cannot impede
   The intellect —

PAULINE   That wood, this grassy bank
   Seem real.

PETER   . . . grass bank. That's it . . . a bank,
   Do you remember?

PAULINE (*eagerly*)   Your snapshot in my locket!
   (*feeling her neck*)
   I left it somewhere.

PETER   Combination lock. . . .
   Four-letter word will turn the secret wards,
   We'll try that key. What are we now but wards
   Of nothing.
                    Come,
                          K

PAULINE   I

PETER   S

PAULINE   S.

   (*They kiss. Stage dims. A rumble of thunder.*)

PAULINE (*withdrawing, alarmed*)   Thunder. . . .
   A flash

PETER   It's going to lash.

PAULINE   Have we done wrong?

PETER   We'll find that shed.
                             The trees are dangerous.
         Keep clear of them.

PAULINE   O what will happen us?

(*They hurry right, up stage. She half turns.*)

My handbag is gone. It vanished from my grasp.

PETER   Don't stop. I'll follow.
                             It must be in the grass.

(*He puts up his coat collar, searches. She runs in,
anguished. He turns to her.*)

PAULINE   Come back. Don't look. . . .

PETER   What is it?

PAULINE   Something hideous.

PETER (*as she drags him away, left*)
         But the rain. You're drenched. You're trembling.
                                   Your mind is hidden.

(*Pause. The sound of heavier rain. Black out.*)

SCENE THREE

(The stage is in darkness. Only Pauline's face can be seen as she kneels at confession. She is murmuring.)

PAULINE   . . . And, Father, I yielded to temptation.

FR. DOYLE   Your boy friend — did he . . .
(*whisper*)

                                        Or attempt to . . .
(*whisper*)

PAULINE   No, Father. I let my handbag fall and
He said he would find it, follow me.
I ran in the rainstorm to a shed
Nearby. . . . Pale, white, as if it had shed
Its fur, a horrible animal
Stood up, with two black paws . . .

(groping for word)

                                        black nimbus.
It glimmered like . . . like . . . a gas-mantle
Turned down. Father, it was a man
With nothing on.

FR. DOYLE (*softly*)   A saint from Hell.

PAULINE   That second, before I could call for help,
I sinned through curiosity.

FR. DOYLE   Did you take pleasure in that impure
Sight, feel desire, my child?

PAULINE   No, I
Was shaking all over.

FR. DOYLE   Would you know him?

28

PAULINE (*suddenly aware of a change in his tone of voice,*
frightened)
How could I?

FR. DOYLE   Look. Do you recognize
Him now?

(*He turns*)

PAULINE   You!
(*in horror*)

FR. DOYLE (*anguished*)   'Spirit that denies.'

(*black out*)
(*drumming*)

SCENE FOUR

(*St. Mary's Place, as Scene One.*)

PAULINE (*off*)
    I'm winning.

    (*runs in. Peter follows.*)

PETER   You see it was nothing but make-believe.
    Not even a cat.

PAULINE   That little rhyme took leave of
    Our senses.

PETER (*presenting it*)
        Your handbag.

PAULINE   That's strange. I must have let
    It fall.
    (*gravely*)
        Peter, I will not write that letter.

PETER (*eagerly*)
    You mean?

PAULINE (*nodding*)
        I'll try now to explain the riddle.
    The first time round, I felt ridiculous.
    Then in the shadows a second time, I wondered
    'What if we really met the Evil One?'
    The third time round I saw Him . . . in a nightmare
    Or trance. Then I was gone from St. Mary's Place.
    In rainy flickers, . . . like . . . like . . . The Living
        Pictures
    At the *Volta*, I saw my own startled features
    As someone, white, red, black-handed, rose from a dark
    Wood, heard my terror calling to you.

30

PETER   Poor darling.

PAULINE (*whispering*)
    The man in the raincoat.
                        No, hiding under that fanlight.

    (*he runs forward, returns*)

PETER   A shadow — trick.

PAULINE   What was I saying?

PETER   You cried out
    For help

PAULINE   More rainy flickers . . . someone crying
    In the dark because she had seen a mortal sin.
    (*confused*)
    The rest is a blank.

PETER   No wonder you feel morbid
    Here in the gloom

PAULINE   I think it was a lesson,
    A hidden fable. Is there more or less on
    The mind, awake or sleeping? You are a student
    And so should know the answer.

PETER   Stewing for
    Examinations: Shakespeare at elbow, sin,
    Bad conscience, hatred — always Elsinore!
    Look how the night has made the Black Church bigger:
    Spire, pinnacle, shadows of bigotry;
    The childish rhyme that runs along those railings,
    There-we-go-round all our elders rail at —
    Thought has its funerals.

PAULINE (*pointing*)   Four men.

PETER (*amused*)   Pall-bearers!

31

PAULINE   They're going down by Granby Row.

PETER   Come, Pauline.

PAULINE (*smiling as she takes his arm*)
You're right, Peter, you have not seen the last
Of me! Some other girl must take that lasting
Vow.

(*As they move upstage, they stop, kiss. They withdraw
suddenly.*)

(*distressed*)
Don't you love me, Peter?

PETER   Your kiss was curt. In
Fact, it
          has
               — can you guess? —
                    brought down the
                              curtain.

(*He points, embarrassed. They steal off. Pause. The
curtain is held. Pause, sound of a horse-and-cab
gradually comes nearer, fades again. Curtain falls.
Immediately Harlequin appears in front of it, masked.*)

HARLEQUIN (*to audience*)
She's in the dressing-room again.
(*peeps through curtain*)
                         There go her stays,
Camisole, lace-trimmed petticoat, and now. . . .
                         What stays me?
(*hesitates*)
I will, I must
(*peeps again*)
          Pierrot is laughing — she's in her drawers
(*turning right*)

32

One moment, please,
(*sotto voce*)
                                    The modest author.
(*dejected*)   I must not draw
Undue attention to them.
(*cautiously glancing, right*)
                                    He borrowed that device
From Blok.
(*complaining*)
                    He knows that voyeurism is my vice.
(*chuckling*)
He thinks his couplets experimental but *rime riche* is
Double-entendre in English. In Irish, plain *arís*
Or, as they say, the same again.
(*unmasking, clears throat*)
                                    But to my piece,
                                                        Though
Mischievous fancy will never leave a fellow in peace,
My wickedness, you see, is really not in earnest
(*peeping through mask*)
Or is it?
                    We laugh, love, sigh, quarrel, bedevil to
                            earn our
Existence, parody your worst thoughts.
(*miming*)   'Harlequin,
He knows about us?'
                    'Nonsense, my dear'
                                    'He found this sequin
Of yours down my corsage.'
(*confidentially*)
                                    Why did I scare Pierrette
Before this comedy began? I want to appear in
Her dreams to-night. In sleep, your world is willy-
            nilly

And virtuous. 'I won't' quickly becomes 'I will'.
Pleasure is in the affirmative. Can she refuse?
Such goings-on are typical, but only a few
Of us are left! The Doctor rapping his spectacle-case,
With breech-charge, clyster, peering down at a comely
        case —
Where is he? And where are Brighetta, the Clown and
        Scaramouche,
Old Pantaloon, the bragging Captain whose only scar
        mouched
Behind? Our lovers would be human, she — more,
        he — less.
Religion was the co-respondent.
(*turning to curtain*)
                                Pin up your lesson,
Pierrette. No . . . stop. It shows too much.
                            Pierrot, the blockhead,
Sulked in that play last week by Alexander Blok.
All symbolism, set in the winter-time —
(*aside*)   White Russia.
White in that whiteness, unseen, a snowstorm had
        rushed
Him off on a sledge in cold pursuit of Columbine.
I waited, cutely, in the scene-dock, to kiss, to coll
His wife.
(*chuckling*)
                That Columbine was only made of cardboard
And when he clasped her, bosom gave no cardiac
Response.
                Later he found us together in a low dive.
Your snow-man cleared the counter. I held Pierrette,
        We dived,
We ducked a ducking.
(*rubbing his head*)

34

I felt an icy blow.

                              Bar, cellar,

Grating, were gone. I woke in Basle —

                              Or Barcelona.

(*shrugging*)
I simply had to. We are international types
Not local. Remelt the metal, font of fire — typesetting
Can never change our mould. *Commedia dell' arte*
Still carries on. The centuries have made us artful.
C'est tout.

            Before I leap Fitzwilliam flights to my attic
And Georgian mug of milk—let's see what they are at.

(*He turns, mimes the withdrawing of the curtain. It
obeys him and he leaves, right.*)

EPILOGUE

(*The dressing-room. Pierrot is sitting on chair in his white costume, pulling up his socks. Pierrette is behind screen changing into her own costume.*)

PIERRETTE (*calling*)
Pierrot . . . Pierrot.

(*she backs out*)

Fasten my bodice, please.

PIERROT   Could hungry suitor refuse so sweet a plea?

(*He fastens hooks and eyes.*)

PIERRETTE (*turning*)
Back to pure whiteness, back to abstract type
Again.

PIERROT   I'm free of collar, bone-stud, tie-pin.

PIERRETTE   Those tiresome human beings —

PIERROT   Unhappy, tormented
By conscience,

PIERRETTE   Fear of sin.

PIERROT   A lamentable
Condition.

PIERRETTE   Someone is listening.
(*she tiptoes up stage*)

Harlequin . . .
He's gone.
(*indignantly*)
Last week, he told me to take quinine,
Hot baths.

36

PIERROT   He's jealous.
                      L-O . . . When we are on our own —

PIERRETTE   I'll cook our supper.

PIERROT   Macaroni.

PIERRETTE   A flask . . .

PIERROT   Chianti.

PIERRETTE   Enormous hunks of bread.

PIERROT   Wide-open mouths.

PIERRETTE   Italians are so ill-bred.

PIERROT (*miming*)
    Next, I'll invent and switch an electric blanket —

PIERRETTE   On!

PIERROT   Off!

PIERRETTE (*softly*)
            And then —

PIERROT   The rest will be a blank!

(*She smiles pertly, runs behind screen, brings back a small music-box and puts it on chair. To its tinkling tone, they trip off. Pause. As the music plays on, the curtain descends slowly.*)

THE THIRD KISS by Austin Clarke is the Twenty-Fourth
Dolmen Edition. The book, designed by Liam Miller,
is set in Pilgrim type and printed and published at
The Dolmen Press, North Richmond Street, Dublin 1,
in the Republic of Ireland. The book was seen through
the press by Liam Browne, the compositor was Jim Hughes
and the pressman was Garrett Doyle. The edition is limited
to five hundred copies.

September 1976.

*Distributed in the U.S.A. and in Canada by
Humanities Press Inc.,
171 First Avenue, Atlantic Highlands, N.J. 07716.*